TEACHERS
TOUCH
ETERNITY!

One Heart at a Time

Ruth Geisler

Teachers Touch Eternity!
One Heart at a Time

Ruth Geisler

ISBN 1-933234-07-5

Copyright © 2005 CTA, Inc.
1625 Larkin Williams Rd., Fenton, MO 63026-1205.

Table of Contents

Dear Teacher,

Get ready to touch hearts—for all eternity. A big order? For you and me, absolutely. But not for our heavenly Father!

God has given you one of the highest honors he gives human beings—the joyful task of sharing the Good News of salvation in his Son, Jesus, with the students he gathers around you.

Whether you are teaching Sunday school, vacation Bible school, a midweek class, a youth Bible study, or classes in a Christian day school, God's Holy Spirit is equipping you with the faith, energy, creativity, and words you need to accomplish his will.

God bless you as you touch eternity—
one heart at a time!

How Did I Get into This?

Read Ephesians 2:8–10.

It's already midnight, and I still have sixteen crosses to cut out . . .
What if they all just give me a glassy-eyed stare and don't say a thing . . .

Don't worry. You're not in this gig alone. God has made you his own through his sacrifice of love on Calvary's cross. What's more, he has equipped you "to do good works, which [he] prepared in advance for [you] to do" (Ephesians 2:10).

God knew, even before you were born, that you would be teaching this class. He will hold your hand as you meet the students he has assembled for you to teach. He will open not only their ears and minds, but also their hearts so that they will remember your words and actions and make them a part of their walk with Jesus.

> ### Pray
> Father, help me to approach my new class with the love and confidence that your Spirit gives me. In Jesus' name. Amen.

You were asked to teach. God led you to say yes. He has given you a lifetime of growing in his Word, faith testing, prayers answered, doubts untangled, and blessings received to share with your students. This experience will be a time of growth and joy for you and for them.

Finish planning and get a good night's sleep. God picked you. He picked a winner.

• TOUCH A HEART TODAY •
BEFORE YOU GO TO SLEEP, READ THE NAME OF EACH STUDENT
IN YOUR CLASS. ASK GOD TO OPEN THAT PERSON'S HEART TO YOUR TEACHING.

First Day of Teaching

Read Isaiah 6:8.

"We need teachers for vacation Bible school," Pastor Dave said at the 9:30 service.

"We need teachers for vacation Bible school," Harry Walton called from the coffee and doughnut table in the courtyard.

"We need vacation Bible school teachers," Isaiah said. Well, not exactly. What Isaiah said was, "I heard the voice of the Lord saying, 'Whom shall I send? And who will go for us?' And I said, 'Here am I. Send me.'"

Pray

Father, thank you for first days. Thank you for the chance to share your life-giving Word with new students. Give me and my students a wide-eyed, first-day expectancy each day we learn together. In Jesus' name. Amen.

When God speaks to you like that, his Holy Spirit has a way of making excuses disappear. Now I stand before a group of nine-year-olds—all wearing bright orange Sonshine T-shirts, all staring at me with veiled eyes, daring me to entertain them in a hot church basement when they'd rather be playing outside.

I breathe a silent prayer, pull my Smiley Guy puppet onto one hand, and do the job God sent me to do.

"Hey, you guys, have I got Good News for you. You are the coolest kids on the planet. God loves you so much he sent his only Son to live and die for you. Fasten your seatbelts and get ready for a wild ride."

The kids giggle and stare at me wide-eyed. I hand out stickers and markers and ask them to design name tags showing what they like best about themselves. The first day has begun.

• TOUCH A HEART TODAY •

WHO IS THE PERSON MOST RESPONSIBLE FOR MOTIVATING YOU TO TAKE ON YOUR TEACHING TASK? CALL THAT PERSON AND SAY THANK YOU.

I Can't Remember Their Names

Read Isaiah 49:16.

Nicole. Nikki. Nicolette. Don't these kids' parents have any imagination? Chloe looks just like Jordan. I've already called each of them by the wrong name twice.

The boys seem easier to remember somehow. Matthew has a buzz cut. Rafael's thick, curly eyelashes are wasted on a boy. Taylor Jack rarely sits still.

I struggle to remember my kids' names during the first few days I teach them. I practice matching their names and faces in my mind. It makes me thankful for the one who will never forget me.

"See, I have engraved you on the palms of my hands," my Father tells me (Isaiah 49:16). It is because of the nail scars engraved in his Son's hands that God holds me so close.

It is this sacrificial love that I want to impart to my students. God can tell Chloe from Jordan and Rafael from Taylor Jack with certainty. He knows how many hairs are on each head, how many beautiful eyelashes surround Rafael's eyes. He has called me to share his faith-giving love with them.

Pray

Father, thank you for keeping my face ever before you. Help me learn my students' names. Help me model your personal love to each of them. In Jesus' name. Amen.

Calling each child by the correct name is the first step in establishing a close relationship with that child. A relationship that allows me to share my own faith. A relationship that helps me show Jesus reaching out with open arms—calling each child by name.

• TOUCH A HEART TODAY •
WRITE THE NAME OF ONE OF YOUR STUDENTS ON A SCRAP OF PAPER AND HOLD IT IN YOUR HAND WHILE YOU PRAY FOR THAT CHILD. PRAY FOR A DIFFERENT CHILD EACH DAY.

9

Kiana Looks So Sad

Read Psalm 139:1–6.

Kiana looks so sad every Sunday. She often rests her head on the table, unwilling to make eye contact with me. I touch her shoulder sometimes while she's making her craft and ask her how she's doing. She flicks her eyes up at me and then stares at her marker-colored project. "I'm okay," she whispers.

Kiana isn't okay. What is making her not okay? Divorce? Abuse? Neglect? Shyness? Fear? What can I do? Should I talk to her mother? to my pastor?

If only I could know Kiana as well as God knows her, as well as he knows me. "LORD, you have searched me and you know me. You know when I sit and when I rise; you perceive my thoughts from afar" (Psalm 139:1–2).

Pray

Father, protect the Kianas in my class. Help me to learn their needs and know how to help them. In Jesus' name. Amen.

I determine to learn Kiana's thoughts, to learn what is happening around her and to her when she sits and when she rises. More and more my teaching is directed at Kiana— always talking with the whole class, always taking time to look right at Kiana.

"Jesus knows all about you and loves you just as you are," I say. "There is no problem too big or little for him to handle. He loves you so much he died on the cross for you. He knows just what you're thinking and just how to help you."

Weeks go by and Kiana begins to sit up and listen. I touch her shoulder and ask if she'd like to talk a minute after Sunday school. She looks me in the eye and says, "Yes."

• TOUCH A HEART TODAY •
IS ANY STUDENT IN YOUR CLASS LOOKING A LITTLE DOWN?
ASK THAT CHILD IF YOU CAN PRAY TOGETHER.

Meeting the Parents

Read Ephesians 6:4.

The children shoot out the door, and I try to get to know their parents as they pick them up.

△ Mrs. Cree grabs Justin's hand and takes off at a run. "Hurry up, you've got a soccer game in ten minutes."

△ Mrs. Warrren has a McDonald's bag in her hand. She and Sally Jean sit down on a bench to eat before they take off for dance class.

△ Mr. Drew pops in the door and calls out, "Earth to Kelly. Hurry up." Kelly looks around her, quickly picking up her lesson leaflet and sweater.

△ Mr. Lee bows at me and smiles as he takes his daughter's hand. "Thank you for loving my Helen."

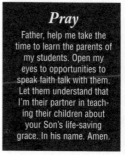

Pray

Father, help me take the time to learn the parents of my students. Open my eyes to opportunities to speak faith talk with them. Let them understand that I'm their partner in teaching their children about your Son's life-saving grace. In his name. Amen.

I realize that I am an extension of each of these parents. God has told them, "Bring [your children] up in the training and instruction of the Lord" (Ephesians 6:4). How do they do that, between the soccer games and the dance classes, daycare and homework? TV and computer games teach ungodly lessons. News programs headline a terrifying, ugly world.

I depend on God's help to make my classroom a haven for my students, a place of grace where only loving lessons are taught. I want it to be a sanctuary where children of divorce, violence, and the daily rush of living can learn these truths: Jesus holds them in his hands. Jesus picked them before they were born to be his own. He led a perfect life in their place and died to win forgiveness for the things they do wrong. They live in the sure promise of Jesus' friendship on earth and his eternal love in heaven.

I shake Mr. Lee's hand. "Let me tell you about the beautiful prayer Helen prayed today."

• TOUCH A HEART TODAY •
HOW CAN YOU SPEAK WORDS OF ENCOURAGEMENT AND SUPPORT TO
EACH STUDENT'S FAMILY THIS WEEK?

Preparing Takes So Long

Read Isaiah 40:28–31.

I've got many things to do on the weekend. The house doesn't clean itself. Only techies grocery shop online. Nobody's got clean clothes. Then there are the games, practices, birthday parties, pizza celebrations, and church functions. What's a teacher to do?

My teacher guide mocks me from the kitchen table. I glance at it guiltily as I run a Swiffer cloth over the television screen. Oh, we do get a clear picture. I knock the lesson guide crooked as I grab my keys to run out the door on endless errands, deliveries, and pick-ups.

Pray

Father, it's so hard to find time to fit everything in. Forgive me when I think of teaching your children as only one more extra task to accomplish. Fill me with your Spirit's strength that I may prepare thoroughly and teach joyfully. In Jesus' name. Amen.

Saturday night, thinking longingly of a hot shower and bed, I sit down at the kitchen table and pull the guide and my Bible close to me. I touch the worn cover of the Bible and open to the passage I need to hear. "He gives strength to the weary. . . . Those who hope in the LORD will renew their strength. They will soar on wings like eagles; they will run and not grow weary, they will walk and not be faint" (Isaiah 40:29–31).

The words take away my guilt over waiting until the last minute to prepare. God gives me a second wind, and I open the guide and begin to study. Time stands still as I prepare to teach God's timeless promises to his children. Ideas begin to pop. If it's a nice day, we could do our lesson outside. I could divide the kids into prayer partners. We could make thank-you cards for our pastor.

Finally I close the guide and put my materials into my canvas bag. A little weary, yes, but still ready to soar like an eagle.

• TOUCH A HEART TODAY •

THINK OF SOMEONE YOU KNOW WHO SPENDS LONG HOURS SERVING THE LORD. SEND THAT PERSON A NOTE OR AN E-MAIL WITH THE WORDS OF ISAIAH 40:28–31. THANK THEM AND LET THEM KNOW YOU ARE PRAYING THAT GOD WILL GIVE THEM REST AND STRENGTH.

She Never Returns My Scissors

Read Ephesians 4:1–6.

That woman next door makes me crazy. She pops in and asks to borrow my scissors. Do they come back? No. Then I'm trying carefully to pull apart the kids' projects without ripping them. She sends a student over for yellow construction paper. Is she familiar with the words "teachers' supply room"?

I look at my students, carefully cutting crosses out of yellow construction paper (which I got out of the supply room this morning). On the crosses they write today's Bible verse. "Be patient, bearing with one another in love" (Ephesians 4:2).

I have to laugh. God certainly uses his Word to teach me what I need to know. I think of the patience God has shown me. He's forgiven me time and time again through the life-giving sacrifice of his Son. He's held me in his arms when life is rough and there's no one to turn to but him. He's listened to me crank and complain instead of thanking him for his generous blessings.

> ## Pray
> Father, give me patience when the people I serve beside annoy me. Remind me that we are about the same work—teaching the peace-giving love won for us through your Son. In his name. Amen.

The woman next door sends a kid over to borrow black markers. "Sure, hon," I say. "I'll pick them up later."

God's Spirit has bonded that woman next door to me in peace. We have one Lord, one faith, one means of eternal life. I can get my scissors later, too.

• TOUCH A HEART TODAY •

DOES SOMEONE YOU WORK WITH ANNOY YOU? PRAY ABOUT YOUR FEELINGS.
ASK GOD TO GIVE YOU STRENGTH TO BE PLEASANT AND OPEN WITH THAT PERSON.
TRY TALKING TOGETHER THE NEXT TIME YOU MEET.

Are They Learning Anything?

Read Colossians 1:9–12.

Taylor is drawing Spiderman webs all around his lesson book. Payton asks to go to the bathroom every ten minutes. Grant and Carson are still sulking after I interrupted their pushing match.

Are these kids learning anything? I want to shout at them. I want to tell them we're dealing with life-saving stuff here and they'd better sit up and pay attention. I want to tell them that if Jesus can hang on the cross and die for them, the least they can do is listen to his Word for a minute.

> ## Pray
> Father, thank you for each of my students. Help me look through the whispering and daydreaming and see the faith miracles that you are working in each heart. In Jesus' name. Amen.

His Word. My anger is turning God's Word inside out, turning God's loving Good News of salvation into angry Law. What God's Word tells me to do is pray for these kids, even thank him for these kids.

My voice is almost a whisper. "I want to tell you something special." I look each student in the eye and say his or her name. Magically, the kids hold still and stare at me. "I pray for each one of you every day. I thank God that you're learning more about him all the time and that your faith is growing all the time. I'm going to start looking for ways you share his love with me and with each other."

We go on with our lesson. I thank Anniken for sharing her faith so beautifully when she leads the class in prayer. "Good going, guys," I compliment Grant and Carson when they manage to pass out the Bibles without starting a civil war. "I thank God each day for you," I honestly tell each child as we say good-bye.

• TOUCH A HEART TODAY •

WRITE A NOTE TO THE PARENTS OF A STUDENT IN YOUR CLASS WHO IS LIVING OUT A LOVING FAITH IN JESUS. TELL THEM YOU THANK GOD THEIR CHILD IS IN YOUR CLASS.

"Jesus Is Cool, Isn't He?"

Read Matthew 18:1–3.

The kids file out the door, and I begin to pick up pencils and forgotten lesson books. Jill walks up to me and says, "Jesus is really cool, isn't he?"

"Oh, yes, Jill. He really is." I hug her in wonder. I know Jill's parents. They're "good" people, but they're not Christians. They're using my services basically as a baby-sitter. Probably the only time Jill has ever heard the name Jesus is when it has been spoken as a profanity. Until my class.

Pray

Father, thank you so much for sending your Spirit into the hearts and minds of my students. It is an unbelievable honor to be your instrument in winning new souls for heaven. Give me a childlike faith that trusts you completely as I carry out my task. In Jesus' name. Amen.

I collapse in a chair, dumbfounded at the experience God has just given me. The long hours of preparation. The annoyance of buying materials from cotton balls to flower pots. The feelings of frustration that I'm not getting through in a meaningful way to the kids' hearts.

All that is now blown away as I realize that God's Spirit has spoken through me to touch the heart of a child. A child who has never heard about Jesus changing water into wine or feeding more than 5,000 people or dying on the cross for her salvation has opened her heart to him in faith.

"Jesus is really cool." Jill spoke with the simple honesty of a child. Her faith was wide-eyed and accepting, as trusting as that of the little child whom Jesus pulled in front of his disciples when they questioned their pecking order in his kingdom.

"Thank you, God," I whisper. My own faith has been touched in a way that it never has. Eagerly I clean up and begin preparing for the next lesson. God's Spirit is using me as a tool to share the life-saving Gospel of Jesus. My teaching is making a difference in kids' lives. As I work, I pray about the words I'll use when I call Jill's parents to tell them what happened.

Jesus is really cool, isn't he?

• TOUCH A HEART TODAY •

SHARE A FAITH-TOUCHING EXPERIENCE YOU'VE HAD IN YOUR CLASSROOM WITH ANOTHER TEACHER. PRAY TOGETHER THAT GOD WILL CONTINUE TO USE YOU TO WIN SOULS FOR HIS KINGDOM.

When the Superintendent Pops In

Read Matthew 5:48.

The superintendent walks in. I stop breathing.

"I'll pop in and out to see how you're doing," our superintendent had told us. "Don't think I'm judging you. I just want to enjoy what's going on and help you in any way I can."

Still forgetting to take a deep breath, I silently thank God that all the kids are sitting down and participating in our discussion. Everything has to go perfectly, or I'll look like I'm not doing my job well. The kids sense my uptightness and tense up, too. They sit a little straighter and try as hard as they can to come up with the right answers.

Pray

Father, thank you for sending your Son to live the perfect life that I cannot live. Fill me with your Spirit's strength so I can model your perfect love for my students. In Jesus' name. Amen.

What is it about being watched by a supervisor that is so threatening? We naturally feel as if we're being judged. We want to be absolutely perfect. Even God's Son tells us, "Be perfect . . . as your heavenly Father is perfect" (Matthew 5:48).

As Jesus taught these words to his listeners in the Sermon on the Mount, he was teaching them about a new kind of love—a perfect love that calls us to love even our enemies. It's a tall order. But it's the standard God holds us to. It's a standard that our first parents, Adam and Eve, failed miserably to uphold. And it's a standard that we fail to measure up to today.

Only God is perfect. It is his perfect love for us that caused him to send his only Son to live a perfect life in our place on earth. Then he sent his Son to the cross to suffer the punishment for the countless times we fail to measure up to his perfect standard. Now God looks at us through the saving love of his Son and sees perfect children.

My superintendent smiles and gives me a high sign and leaves the room. I remember to breathe again. It was a perfect visit.

· TOUCH A HEART TODAY ·

LET YOUR SUPERVISOR KNOW THAT YOU'RE PRAYING FOR HIM OR HER.

Open My Heart:

Prayer and Journal Time

In three of the hearts on this page, jot down three ways in which you feel God blessing your teaching. In three other hearts, write three ways in which you'd like your teaching to improve. Then take your thanks and your requests to God in prayer.

They Got It Today!

Read 2 Timothy 4:7–8.

What a blast! Their hands were waving in the air. They couldn't wait to share their ideas about heaven.

"It's like making every goal you kick in soccer and the guys carry you on their shoulders," Kalei said.

"It's like Disneyland and Christmas and your birthday every day," Emma shared.

"Yes, yes," I said. "But what is it, exactly, that makes heaven so wonderful?"

Karina shot straight up from her chair, following her raised hand. "It's wonderful because you're with Jesus all the time."

"That's it!" I almost shouted. "Heaven is being with Jesus all the time. It's better than soccer and pizza and streets made of solid gold and Disneyland and anything else you can think of."

Pray

Father, thank you so much for the times when things go well in my class. Keep my students motivated to learn more and more about their Savior. Thank you for sending Jesus to run the race of faith with me. Thank you that he has already won me the crown of eternal life. In his name. Amen.

Julia waved her hand. "You're always saying Jesus is with us all the time. So is heaven sort of starting now?"

I smiled. "Heaven will be way better than earth, because there will be no sin or sadness or sickness or loneliness. But our eternal life has already started. We live in the peace and joy of Jesus right now, and when we die, we'll wake up with him in heaven."

The hour had flown by, the kids more excited about their faith than I had ever seen them. I breathed a silent thank-you to God. He'd helped me run a good race, fight a good fight. The victorious crown was mine!

• TOUCH A HEART TODAY •

CATCH SOME OF YOUR STUDENTS OUTSIDE CLASS AND TELL THEM
HOW MUCH THEIR FAITH SHARING MEANS TO YOU.

I'm Ready—before Midnight!
Read Psalm 9:1–2.

My plans are done! The craft is ready. The kids are in bed. The dishwasher is running. It's only nine o'clock!

I rejoice with David, "I will praise you, O LORD, with all my heart; I will tell of all your wonders. I will be glad and rejoice in you; I will sing praise to your name, O Most High" (Psalm 9:1–2).

Pray
Father, thank you for guiding my preparation and teaching. Thank you for showering me with blessings large and small. In Jesus' name. Amen.

What a blessing to have some free time. What a blessing to feel totally ready. I flip through a magazine and run a hot bath. I do have much to rejoice about—much more than a free hour or two. God fills every hour of my life with wonder. I take time to thank God for my many blessings—my family, home, friends, good health, and the bright sunshine today. The enormity of what God has done for me makes it possible for me to revel in such small things.

My thoughts come full circle. I remember the lesson I've planned for tomorrow. We will be talking about the blessings God gives us. Free time will certainly be on our list. But we'll also list freedom for all time—freedom to celebrate sins forgiven because of Jesus' sacrifice on the cross. Freedom to enjoy the small blessings of day-to-day living because of the large blessing of eternal life.

I fall into bed and close my eyes. Yes. I'm ready.

• TOUCH A HEART TODAY •

DO YOU KNOW SOMEONE WHO IS STRUGGLING RIGHT NOW? IT MAY BE HARD FOR THAT PERSON TO ENUMERATE AND APPRECIATE GOD'S BLESSINGS IN THE FACE OF HIS PROBLEMS. GIVE HIM A CALL AND ASK IF YOU CAN PRAY TOGETHER.

I Love Talking to Roxanne

Read 1 Corinthians 12:26.

Ilove talking to Roxanne. It feels like she's an extension of myself. She always knows exactly what to say.

If the kids are bouncing off the walls and driving me nuts, she jokes me down. If I'm struggling, she'll suggest we go for coffee. We talk out the problem. She helps me list options, and we pray together.

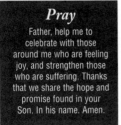

Pray

Father, help me to celebrate with those around me who are feeling joy, and strengthen those who are suffering. Thanks that we share the hope and promise found in your Son. In his name. Amen.

When I think of Roxanne, I remember Paul's words describing the church as one body. "If one part suffers, every part suffers with it; if one part is honored, every part rejoices with it" (1 Corinthians 12:26).

Christ is the head of our body—the one who joins us together in his saving love. Roxanne isn't an extension of me; she's an extension of Christ. Sometimes God calls me to be a Roxanne (or little Christ) to others. When my sister calls to tell me she's expecting twins, it's easy. When Ellen tells me the cancer has spread to her lymph nodes, or Ray tells me he and Linda are thinking of separating, it's much harder.

When someone in the church—my body—suffers, I naturally suffer, too. It is then that I turn to the head of my body. Jesus reminds me that my friends' suffering is never God's will. Suffering is a result of sin in the world. Jesus suffered all the pain for that sin when he gave his life for us on the cross.

I can tell Ellen that Jesus suffered the pain of cancer; Ray, that Jesus felt the sting of considering divorce during his agony on Good Friday. I can tell them that Jesus holds them close, that he will comfort and guide them as he leads them through earthly troubles to an eternity of peace and joy.

I'm no Roxanne. But Jesus helps me hold my own.

• TOUCH A HEART TODAY •
WHO IS YOUR ROXANNE? CALL AND PLAN A COFFEE DATE—ON YOU!

This Isn't What I Planned!

Read Proverbs 16:9.

"Good morning," I say. "Today we'll be learning about the first miracle Jesus did when he lived on earth."

Janeen is waving her hand in the air. "Yes, Janeen?"

"Did you hear about that boy who was killed last night? They said it might be part of an initiation into a satanic cult. How can anybody worship Satan?"

I sigh. "I can't say, Janeen. It seems impossible to me. But we have to remember that ever since God created the world, Satan has been trying every trick he's got to get people on his side. Maybe when some people feel hopeless or don't believe in God, they're drawn in by Satan instead."

I look to the back of the room in surprise. Reticent R.J. is holding his hand a couple of inches away from his lap. He looks down at his black T-shirt and mumbles, "You know how people say that playing Dungeons and Dragons and dumb stuff like that can lead you to follow Satan? Do you believe that kind of stuff?"

> ### Pray
> Father, give me the wisdom to know when to abandon my plans and teach my students what they desperately need to know. In Jesus' name. Amen.

I may have planned to teach about the wedding at Cana, but God knows R.J. needs to know that he belongs solely to his Savior. "That's a good question, R.J.," I say, "and a difficult one. Some people say that getting too fascinated with things like wizardry and magic can lead people to witchcraft or satanism. But remember that Satan can trick us in many ways. A famous writer named C. S. Lewis said the one thing Satan loves the most is when we become so frightened by him that we think about him all the time. You don't need to worry about Satan gaining control over you. Jesus already defeated him by dying on the cross in your place. You belong to Jesus. He bought you with his own blood. No one will snatch you out of his hands."

It's not what I planned, but what God knew the kids needed.

• TOUCH A HEART TODAY •
DOES ANY STUDENT IN YOUR CLASS SEEM DESPONDENT OR TROUBLED?
PLAN A WAY TO GET CLOSE TO THAT STUDENT.

"You're the Best Teacher Ever!"

Read 2 Corinthians 3:2–3.

We are closing our lesson books and getting out glue bottles and scissors to make our craft. Out of nowhere Rafaella raises her hand and exclaims, "You're the best teacher ever!"

I smile and say, "Thank you, Rafaella. You are a great student."

Pray

Father, thank you for using my teaching as a tool for your Holy Spirit. Let the world clearly read my students' words and behavior as letters from your Son. In his name. Amen.

It's easy to start feeling pretty good about my teaching when kids like Rafaella give such loving testimonials. But I know the impact of my teaching doesn't rest with me at all.

"You yourselves are our letter, written on our hearts, known and read by everybody," Paul told the Corinthians. "You show that you are a letter from Christ, the result of our ministry, written not with ink but with the Spirit of the living God, not on tablets of stone but on tablets of human hearts" (2 Corinthians 3:2–3).

Rafaella speaks so lovingly, not because of my ability as a teacher, but because she is learning to share the love of Jesus. God's Holy Spirit is working through our lessons, my words, the children's sharing of their faith, to turn Rafaella into a little letter from Christ.

I decide to share my thoughts with the class. "You know, every one of you is like a letter Jesus writes to the world. When you tell other people about Jesus and share his love with them, you are like a letter God is writing to them about Jesus."

Naturally Sky is the first to speak up. "I don't think I'd fit into a mailbox."

This is great first-grade humor that cracks up the class. I smile. "We don't want you in a mailbox, Sky. We want you out in the world, sharing your love for Jesus."

Rafaella. Sky. Each sweet little face a letter from Christ. I thank God for them.

• TOUCH A HEART TODAY •

HOW DO YOUR STUDENTS SHOW THAT THEY ARE LETTERS FROM CHRIST?
BEGINNING TODAY, WRITE A NOTE TO ONE STUDENT A DAY, THANKING THEM
FOR THE WAY THEY SHARE THEIR FAITH.

Cody Falls out of His Chair

Read 1 Corinthians 10:12–13.

Cody is diligently coloring a picture of Jesus the Good Shepherd. His knees are planted on his chair so he can lean across the table and get just the color he needs for the verdant green pastures. He leans to his right to color the bottom edge of the picture. "Be careful, Cody, you're going to fall out of your—"

Pray

Father, temptations to worry, act spitefully, and forget your presence assail me from every direction. Thank you for promising to uphold me in your love. In Jesus' name. Amen.

Too late! Cody is on the floor. He climbs back in his chair with a sheepish grin. Cody is a wiggle worm. He falls out of his chair regularly. It exasperates me and I want to snap at him.

Impatient behavior toward my students is only one of the temptations I face daily. There's the teacher who has something negative to say at every meeting. I want to snap at her in the same negative tone.

And there are bigger things to face—like my dad falling deeper into Alzheimer's dense fog. How can I continue to care for him? It's painful just to see him. There's my son wanting to borrow the car every five minutes. He's had some close calls. I'd like to lock him in his room until he's 36.

I remember the verses I have written on a card on my refrigerator. "So, if you think you are standing firm, be careful that you don't fall! No temptation has seized you except what is common to man. And God is faithful; he will not let you be tempted beyond what you can bear. But when you are tempted, he will also provide a way out so that you can stand up under it" (1 Corinthians 10:12–13).

Cody will continue to fall out of his chair, and I will continue to worry about life's problems. But God is holding me up in his strong arms. He will not let me fall away from him. I stand firm in God-given faith. Now if Cody could just stay in his chair . . .

• TOUCH A HEART TODAY •

DO YOU KNOW A COLLEAGUE WHO IS DEALING WITH A DIFFICULT PERSONAL PROBLEM THAT MAY CAUSE DESPAIR? CALL THAT PERSON AND LET HER KNOW YOU ARE PRAYING FOR HER.

Are They Getting It?

Read Isaiah 55:11.

The kids walk in, and Brent gives Caitlyn a shove. Caitlyn laughs and shoves him back. I decide to ignore it.

We begin our devotion, and I see Kendra doodling on her lesson book. Austin looks furtively at me as he tries to sneak his iPod plug into his ear. I glare at him, and he sticks the cord back in his pocket.

Are these kids getting anything out of class? I see no change in their behavior, no interest in learning anything about God's Word.

Yet God promises me, "[My Word] will not return to me empty, but will accomplish what I desire" (Isaiah 55:11). I'm not the only one working in this room. The Holy Spirit is at work in these kids' hearts. Caitlyn may look like she's not interested, but who knows when something she has learned in Bible class will give her comfort in a troubled time.

Pray

Father, give me courage when the kids I'm teaching don't seem to be getting it. Fill my heart and mind with patience and innovation, and fill their hearts and minds with openness to your Word. In Jesus' name. Amen.

Austin is definitely too cool for school, yet God's Spirit can set his heart on fire with faith in his Lord. I continue to teach, and slowly the kids begin to listen and participate. Brent raises his hand and asks what I think about kids who are hooked on drugs. Do they have a chance of being saved?

"Of course," I say. "Jesus' love is much stronger than any drug."

Hands begin to wave and "What ifs?" fill the room. These kids seem to be getting it.

• TOUCH A HEART TODAY •

THINK OF A STUDENT WHO SEEMS TO HAVE BEEN ESPECIALLY TOUCHED BY YOUR TEACHING. GET IN TOUCH WITH THAT STUDENT AND SEE HOW THINGS ARE GOING.

It's Just a Game!

Read 1 Timothy 6:12.

"We won!"

"No! *We* won!"

The kids come in from game time completely unhinged over who won the kick ball game.

"Why don't we call it a tie," I say hopefully. Never one to turn my back on a teaching opportunity, I continue. "You know, living a Christian life is kind of like playing a game or fighting a fight."

"How can that be?" Courtney asks. "Jesus doesn't like us to fight, does he?"

"That's the best part," I answer. "Jesus has already won our fight for us. Paul tells us, 'Fight the good fight of the faith. Take hold of the eternal life to which you were called' (1 Timothy 6:12). Jesus fought our fight and beat the devil for good when he died on the cross for us. Our prize is eternal life with him."

Pray

Father, give me patience when my students fight over trivial things. Thank you for sending your Son to win my fight with sin and Satan for me. In his name. Amen.

"But the devil still tries to get us to sin, right?" Devon asks.

"That's right. But we've got the upper hand. We fight our fight against the devil knowing that Jesus has already won the battle for us."

I continue to teach, firm in my faith that God has sealed my salvation through the sacrifice of his Son. He has done the same for these young battlers I teach.

• TOUCH A HEART TODAY •

IS A STUDENT, FAMILY MEMBER, OR COLLEAGUE CAUGHT UP IN A FAITH BATTLE? OFFER TO STUDY GOD'S WORD AND PRAY WITH THAT PERSON.

I Didn't Volunteer for This Part

Read Luke 17:10.

Paige has been troubled for months. She speaks only when I ask her a direct question. She withdraws from the other kids. Finally the day comes when I dismiss the rest of the class and Paige remains in her chair, arms hugging her chest, rocking back and forth.

I sit beside her and speak gently. "Paige, is there anything you want to tell me?"

Paige's startled eyes widen in fear, and she moves away from me, but only a chair away. She wraps her arms around herself again, not wanting anyone else to see the hurt that is inside.

"Paige, let's talk. Sometimes when we're feeling bad about things, it helps to talk."

Pray

Father, guide me when I get in over my head and find myself involved with things I didn't know I was volunteering for. Let me be your willing servant. In Jesus' name. Amen.

"I can't," Paige whispers. "He said he'd kill my mom and dad if I told."

My stomach flips. I signed on to teach Sunday school. What do I know about the nasty maze of abuse? But Paige has chosen me to trust. "He didn't say he'd kill me," I say firmly. "Tell me what's been happening."

Gradually the maze unravels. My pastor and I talk to Paige's parents. The police get involved. Counselors are called in. One day Paige will feel safe and loved again.

Serving the Lord would be easier if we could take the low road, just doing what's minimally required. But I know Jesus holds me to a higher calling. He tells me, "So you also, when you have done everything you were told to do, should say, 'We are unworthy servants; we have only done our duty'" (Luke 17:10).

I will continue to reach out to Paige or any child Jesus puts in my path. It's part of the job.

• TOUCH A HEART TODAY •

IS ONE OF YOUR COLLEAGUES DEALING WITH A DIFFICULT SITUATION?
CALL AND OFFER TO LISTEN AND PRAY TOGETHER.

What a Teacher Does at Night

Read Psalm 121:1–4.

What do teachers do at night? They wonder if moving Josh across the room from Noah would quiet both boys down. They wonder how in the world they can make the Pentecost story understandable for children. They wonder if there are any craft sticks at church or if they should run out and hunt some down.

Some worries might be closer to home. Why does Chad spend so much time in his room? Has that boy Brooke wants to date served jail time? When can I get to the doctor? These headaches are occurring more often.

Actually, teachers can stop worrying and sleep in peace because someone else is watching the shop. The psalmist counsels, "He who watches over Israel will neither slumber nor sleep" (Psalm 121:4). Our Lord stays awake all night, guarding those we love and standing ready to help us with our worries.

Pray

Father, let me sleep in peace tonight, knowing you are guarding all the details of my life. In Jesus' name. Amen.

What do teachers do at night? They prepare. They pray. Then they sleep, secure in the knowledge that God is wide awake, meeting all their needs.

• TOUCH A HEART TODAY •
WHICH STUDENT ARE YOU WORRYING ABOUT? WHICH FAMILY MEMBER?
INCLUDE THEM IN YOUR BEDTIME PRAYERS.

Open My Heart:

Prayer and Journal Time

*In three of the hearts on this page, write
down three clues that your students' faith is
growing. On other hearts, write down the
names of students who need special help.
Thank God for the good things going on in
your class, and ask God to guide you in
helping the students who need direction.*

Class Is Over!

Read Psalm 118:24.

Class is over. It's been great, but now you can sit down for a moment or chat with a friend or pop open a diet soft drink.

There's nothing quite like the end of a teaching experience to help you savor the psalmist's words, "This is the day the LORD has made; let us rejoice and be glad in it" (Psalm 118:24). Now there is time to think back through what happened and evaluate how things went. No more departing from the lesson plan and taking questions on the fly. No more winging it through unexpected situations.

It's time to thank God for the things that went well—the kids' watching for your cheerful greeting as they enter the room, the times they're wholeheartedly involved in learning God's Word, their prayers that move you to tears.

Pray

Father, thank you for the end of lessons and time to relax and reflect. Thank you for every new tomorrow in Jesus. In his name. Amen.

It's a time to evaluate what to do next. A time to look forward to a fresh beginning. That's one great benefit in living as a child of God. Every day brings a new beginning, no matter that failures, disappointments, and temptations battered us yesterday. Today brings a new day— sins forgiven; hope renewed, reborn by God's grace—a day to rejoice and be glad.

• TOUCH A HEART TODAY •

LEAVE A TREAT ON A COLLEAGUE'S DESK TO ENJOY AFTER CLASS.

Seeing Mikayla in the Grocery Store

Read Hebrews 2:14–18.

"**M**ommy! Mommy! It's my teacher!"

I recognize Mikayla's screech from three aisles away. I glance at my cart. Good. Cereal, lettuce, and milk. No doughnuts or ice cream. At least, none yet. Mikayla and her mom cruise over.

"I'm so sorry," Mikayla's mom says with a smile. "She just loves you. She treats you like a movie star." Mikayla stares at me wide-eyed.

Pray

Father, thank you for sending your Son from the perfection of heaven to live a temptation-filled life on earth and suffer and die for my imperfections. In his name. Amen.

Yes, teachers are human. We eat. Cut us, and we bleed. It's nice to be held up on a pedestal, idolized and worshiped from afar. A Christian teacher can easily portray that image for a child. We know all the answers. Our prayers are well worded and always answered. We know what to say when children celebrate or mourn.

But reality lurks beneath the thin veneer of our perfect spirituality. We actually enjoy ice cream more than lettuce. Thankfully, we do not have to be seen in public when we first get out of bed. Our patience wears thin at red lights, long lines, and rude clerks. There are times when we don't know the right thing to say or do, times when we struggle just to keep going day after day.

These are the times when we hug our Savior in all his humanity close, the Christ who "had to be made like his brothers in every way, in order that he might . . . make atonement for the sins of the people" (Hebrews 2:17).

The Christ who faced every temptation we face, became as tired as we become, and wept in sorrow over lost friends is Jesus, who gave his life for our imperfections. He is a Savior to be hugged close in real life.

• TOUCH A HEART TODAY •

SHARE A PERSONAL FAITH STORY WITH YOUR CLASS. SHOW A PICTURE OF YOUR FAMILY OR PET SO YOUR STUDENTS CAN LEARN ABOUT YOUR EVERYDAY LIFE.

Remember Me?

Read 1 Corinthians 15:58.

"**H**i. Remember me?"

I looked up to see a skinny teenager in hip-hugger jeans and tank top, long dirty-blonde hair framing her face.

I stopped cleaning my classroom and smiled at her. "Give me a hint."

"I'm Jennifer," she said. Instantly I remembered a skinny little first grader with long, lank hair hanging to her shoulders. The absolute only thing I remembered about her was that she cried a lot.

"You mean so much to me," Jennifer said shyly. "I wondered if you might still be here. I think about you all the time."

I've had kids tell me that I've helped their faith grow, that I've helped them become the people they grew to be, that I've helped them decide to enter church work. But Jennifer's words blew me away as none of these high-minded testimonials had. God had helped me make a huge impact on a child I could barely remember.

Pray
Father, help me share your love with all my students in an unforgettable way. In Jesus' name. Amen.

As a teacher you touch every child in your class in ways far beyond your imagination. Your smile, your word of encouragement, your prayer, or your pat on the back may uplift a student and create a memory that will last much longer that you could possibly know.

You are Jesus to your students. Shy Jennifers of all ages and both genders sit before you, waiting for the words and actions that will make their Savior real to them. One day, here on earth or in heaven, a Jennifer will say, "Remember me?" and you will know "that your labor in the Lord is not in vain" (1 Corinthians 15:58).

• T O U C H   A   H E A R T   T O D A Y •

GET IN TOUCH WITH A PREVIOUS STUDENT. FIND OUT WHAT'S HAPPENING AND LET THAT INDIVIDUAL KNOW YOU ARE CONTINUING TO PRAY FOR HIM OR HER.

What Would Mrs. Spenser Do?

Read Hebrews 12:1–2.

Mrs. Spenser was, without a doubt, my favorite Sunday school teacher. When we were in the fifth grade, she invited the five girls in the class to her home one Saturday afternoon. She helped us make pink flannel nightgowns for babies in an orphanage in Mexico.

I've thought in later years about those crooked little nightgowns with unfinished seams and those poor little babies who had to wear them. But Mrs. Spenser touched my life in a way that no other Sunday school teacher had. She invited me into her home. She showed me faith in action. We didn't talk about helping others, we did it.

Now when I'm planning my own lessons, I often think, "What would Mrs. Spenser do—to make the story come alive, to involve the kids in living out their faith, to show Jesus as one who acted on his love?"

Pray

Father, thank you for the vast army of saints who cheer me on from their heavenly home. In Jesus' name. Amen.

The author of Hebrews tells us we are surrounded by a great cloud of witnesses, cheering us on to our victory in heaven. Mrs. Spenser is one of my witnesses. I imagine her voice calling out to me from the saints who surround her. "Get personal with those kids. Show them your own faith. Let them know that Jesus is real in their lives."

With witnesses like Mrs. Spenser cheering us on, we teachers change students' lives. God's Spirit touches students' hearts with our words and actions, just as Mrs. Spenser's touched mine.

I fix my eyes on Jesus, searching for ways to share his saving love with my students. Mrs. Spenser cheers me on.

• TOUCH A HEART TODAY •

DO YOU HAVE A MRS. SPENSER IN YOUR LIFE? LET THAT PERSON KNOW HOW YOU FEEL.

The Parents Don't Know My Name

Read Isaiah 43:1.

I've taught vacation Bible school and Sunday school at this church for five years, and the parents rarely remember my name. They smile kindly when they pick up their kids and go on their way.

I could be offended, but it's okay, really. God knows my name. In fact, he has called me by name to be a worker in his kingdom.

I know it is vital to call my students by name in order to let them know how important they are to me and to Jesus. Calling them by name helps to let them know that God has known them since before they were born and called them to be his own and live in his kingdom.

Pray
Father, thank you for calling me by name to be your own. Don't let lack of recognition in my congregation dim my desire to teach your children. In Jesus' name. Amen.

Maybe God is calling me to send a message to the parents, too. Names are important—in God's eyes and ours. I begin by memorizing my students' last names. One by one I am able to call a parent by name as the class is dismissed.

"You must be Mrs. Sims. It's a delight to have Michael in class."

"Thank you so much," Mrs. Sims says warmly. "Michael thinks the world of you. What is your name again?"

This might just work.

• **TOUCH A HEART TODAY** •
CALL OR E-MAIL THE PARENTS OF ONE OF YOUR STUDENTS. LET THEM KNOW YOU ARE A PARTNER IN HELPING THEIR CHILD GROW IN FAITH.

Where's He Staying Tonight?

Read Matthew 10:29–31.

"Nicky, I have an important note about the church picnic. Are you going home with Mommy or Daddy today?"

"I don't know," Nicky replies. Not concerned, he continues to glue animal crackers on his construction-paper ark. My heart stops, and I bite my lip to hold back tears. I grew up with the certainty that both parents would be at home to care for me each day. How can a child like Nicky be so unworried about where he will spend the night?

Perhaps never knowing what is coming next becomes a way of life. Perhaps Nicky has learned at an early age that worrying doesn't change a thing. Both of his parents love him. One of them will come to pick him up.

It is my job to teach Nicky that he has another parent, a Father who knows him down to the hair count on his head. He has a Father who loves him enough to let his own Son die to win Nicky a sure home in heaven.

"You know what, Nicky? I'll give you one note for Mom and one for Dad. Then I'll see you at the picnic."

• TOUCH A HEART TODAY •
MAKE A POINT TO GIVE SPECIAL COMFORT AND A LISTENING EAR
TO A STUDENT WHO IS GOING THROUGH FAMILY TROUBLES.

May I Hold Your Hand?

Read Psalm 63:8.

"May I hold your hand?" Christy murmurs as she grabs my hand on the way to church. Nothing feels quite as warm as a young child grasping teacher's hand. It brings a spring to your step and a smile to your lips. It lets you know that a child loves you and trusts you completely.

Hand-holding is a universal sign of compassion, caring, and respect in our society. We shake hands upon meeting a stranger. We instinctively reach for a child's hand when crossing the street. Couples of all ages walk hand-in-hand as a sign of tenderness. When visiting a loved one in the hospital, it is only natural to grasp a hand and stroke it. Athletes shake hands at the end of a competition as a sign of good sportsmanship. Business deals are clinched with a handshake. We even teach our dogs to shake hands.

Pray
Father, thank you for firmly grasping my hand in yours. Guide me as I teach your children, and hold me up when I am tired and weak. In Jesus' name. Amen.

Holding hands is also a good reminder of our relationship with our heavenly Father. David says, "My soul clings to you; your right hand upholds me" (Psalm 63:8). David certainly knew the strength of God's right hand holding him up in times of danger, sin, and celebration. He felt God's hand steady his as he slung a stone at the giant Goliath. He clung to God's hand as the Lord led him to victory after victory over Israel's enemies. He felt the heavy hand of God's Law and the merciful hand of his forgiveness when he killed Uriah to take Bathsheba as his wife.

As teachers we cling to God's hand as we prepare our lessons, trusting his Spirit to make our words relevant to our students' lives. We place our hand in God's as we trust in his mercy and compassion in times of doubt and sorrow. God's hand holds us up in victorious times and troubled times. When we question, "May I hold your hand?" his answer is always, "I am already holding yours."

• TOUCH A HEART TODAY •
GIVE SOMEONE'S HAND A SQUEEZE TODAY AND LET THEM KNOW
HOW MUCH YOU LOVE THEM.

Opening the Door

Read John 10:9.

There's nothing like opening the door before class and getting things set up. Everything is possible. You're totally prepared and looking forward to a positive experience. You've opened the door so your students may come in and learn about the one who opened the door to heaven.

When Jesus refers to himself as the Good Shepherd, he says, "I am the gate for the sheep." In biblical times, one important accessory—a gate—was missing from the sheep pen. After the shepherd had carefully counted his sheep and put them safely inside their stone fence, he lay down on the ground to fill the opening. The shepherd was the door to the pen. No wolf or lion could attack his sheep without matching wits with the shepherd first. No lamb could stray away. No thief could make off with part of the flock. The shepherd would lay down his own life for his sheep.

Pray

Father, thank you for sending your Son to open the door to heaven. Help me to speak with the loving words of the Good Shepherd when I teach my students. In his name. Amen.

Our Good Shepherd opened the door to heaven by giving his life on the cross for us. Life is his gift to us, and he himself is life. We get to share the Good News of what Jesus has done for us each time our students enter our classroom door.

Many voices other than the Good Shepherd's tempt our students to enter other doors: Doors that lead to video games glorifying violence. Doors that open to boom boxes screaming the joys of illicit sex in foul words. Doors that reveal plasma TVs purporting to call all manners of assorted people living together "realistic." Doors that make gods of cool clothes and other must-have retail items.

When you open your door, your students hear the voice of the Good Shepherd. This is the Good Shepherd who leads them safely into his fold, guarding them from temptation and danger, and leading them through the door he has opened into eternal life in heaven.

• TOUCH A HEART TODAY •

WRITE AN ENCOURAGING NOTE AND TAPE IT TO A COLLEAGUE'S CLASSROOM DOOR.

Maybe Tomorrow Will Be Different

Read Hebrews 13:8.

My head is pounding. The kids wiggled and whispered through the whole lesson. I'm sure no one learned a thing. Kyle asked to go to the bathroom and proceeded to decorate the ceiling of the church men's room with wads of wet toilet paper.

Pray

Father, sometimes I want to quit. Thank you for never quitting on me. Fill me with your Son's patience, love, and understanding. In his name. Amen.

We Christian teachers have our up days and our down days. Fortunately for us, Jesus Christ is the same yesterday and today and forever. In fact, when we are at our weakest, Jesus is at his strongest. He can work through Kyle's interior-decorating tendencies and touch Kyle's heart with repentance and faith.

Jesus is ready to reach out and refresh you, to remind you that he is teaching right beside you and to assure you that tomorrow will be a better day. Not that he promises you smooth sailing. Jesus asks us to take up our cross and follow him. We will follow him through days mired with illness, financial woes, family stress, and kids bouncing off the walls.

What Jesus does promise us is that he will faithfully hold us by the hand each day. He will listen closely to our prayers and grant us the best possible answers—the things he knows we need even before we ask. He will give us the patience to deal with unruly children and inspire us with ideas to motivate kids to learn the greatest lesson of all: Jesus knew you before you were born. He stands beside you today as your Savior and Friend. Tomorrow he will take you to heaven to live with him forever.

· TOUCH A HEART TODAY ·

IS SOMEONE YOU KNOW HAVING A TOUGH DAY? LET HER KNOW JESUS IS WITH HER.

I Know I Have a Pencil Somewhere

Read 2 Corinthians 5:17.

I hate it when I make a mistake in my lesson plans. I white-out the mistake and blow impatiently on the white blotch, willing it to dry quickly. I start writing again too soon, creating a jagged blue line through white film. Now I add more Liquid Paper, creating a small plaster sculpture on the page, and leave the room until it is thoroughly dry. It might be easier to just write my lesson plans with pencil. I'd have to erase a lot, but the little eraser bits would feel at home living with the dust on the furniture and carpet.

> ### Pray
> Father, forgive me for the many sins I've committed as I've taught. Thank you for forgiving me daily and letting me stand before your children as a new creation. In my Savior's name. Amen.

Mistakes bog teachers down. We spoke impatiently to a child. We coasted through a lesson when we could have taught some energized Gospel. We left planning until the last minute and didn't have time to execute the creative projects that came to mind when we opened the classroom door. We ran the other direction when we saw the talkative, high-maintenance parent approaching. We dwell on our mistakes until all of our teaching seems like one large error.

Thankfully, God doesn't reach for the Liquid Paper or his big eraser. He just transforms us into new creations. "If anyone is in Christ, he is a new creation; the old has gone, the new has come!" (2 Corinthians 5:17). Thanks to Jesus' redeeming work on Calvary our past mistakes and sins are gone—not blocked out, not erased, gone. They no longer exist.

We stand before God and our students as redeemed, forgiven, newly transformed teachers. We freely share the love and forgiveness God has showered on us with our students. We plan lessons with the zest that only the Holy Spirit can give. We prayerfully teach our way into the hearts and minds of children until they, too, are transformed by God's Spirit and live as his new creations.

• TOUCH A HEART TODAY •

TOUCH YOUR OWN HEART TODAY. WRITE DOWN A "TEACHING SIN" THAT YOU HAVE COMMITTED ON A SHEET OF PAPER. CONFESS THE SIN TO GOD AND CELEBRATE HIS FORGIVENESS AS YOU SHRED THE PAPER INTO A WASTEBASKET.

Open My Heart:

Prayer and Journal Time

On several hearts below, write down the names of several parents who uplift you in your faith walk. On other hearts, write the names of some parents who seem to need some help in sharing God's love with their children. Thank God for the parents who build you up, and ask him to help you find ways to motivate the parents who need help.

What If . . .

Read 1 Peter 5:7.

Only the lionhearted discuss fire-drill plans with first graders. "What if a fire starts in our room and we can't get out?" "What if we're standing on the grass and the grass catches on fire?" "What if we're standing on the parking lot and the parking lot catches on fire?" "God wouldn't let the church burn down, would he?" "What if you're going to the bathroom and you aren't done?"

Such discussions end with the teacher saying firmly, "Don't worry. God will keep us safe." But don't our own what-ifs sometimes rival those of first graders? What if I can't make the house payment? What if the rest of the staff thinks less of me because I'm new to the church? What if my latest medical tests are positive? What if my spouse and I can't reconcile the anger we're feeling? What if my daughter starts hanging out with the wrong crowd?

Pray

Father, forgive me when I worry unceasingly. Reassure me with your promise to take care of all my worries. In Jesus' name. Amen.

God heals our what-if disease by taking all the what-ifs on himself. "Cast all your anxiety on him because he cares for you" (1 Peter 5:7). Satan sends anxiety and worry to eat at the foundation of our faith. We can easily get caught up in full-time worrying, sleepless nights of worrying, days so fraught with worrying that we hardly know what we're doing.

The antidote for worry is prayer. God stands with open arms, ready to take every worry and what-if we bring him. He promises to deal with our problems in the best way and the best time—his way and his time. We can continue our lives, refreshed with hope and new possibilities.

• TOUCH A HEART TODAY •

ASK A COLLEAGUE TO BE A PRAYER WARRIOR WITH YOU. PRAY FOR AND ABOUT EACH OTHER'S WORRIES. THEN LET GOD HANDLE THEM.

"You Can't Come to My Birthday Party!"

Read Ephesians 4:32.

It doesn't take much of a slight for one child to yell at another, "You can't come to my birthday party!" or "You can't play with us anymore!" or "You're a big baby!"

Although adults rarely get to the point of yelling, "You can't come to my birthday party," we can easily fall into the temptation of thinking some pretty insulting things about one another. Why can't that teacher get to class on time? I'm tired of having to settle his kids down and watch my own class at the same time.

We can even get to the point where we unin-vite ourselves to our own birthday party. Why did I say that to Mrs. Paige? She'll think I'm an idiot. Why can't I remember to bring everything I need to class? I'm so stupid.

Pray

Father, forgive my students when they put each other down. Forgive me when I am unkind to others and to myself. Help me to share your Son's compassion and forgiveness. In his name. Amen.

God puts an end to all birthday-party uninviting through the work of his Son. "Be kind and compassionate to one another, forgiving each other, just as in Christ God forgave you" (Ephesians 4:32). When children bicker, we can sit down with them and talk things out. We can brainstorm better ways to handle the matter next time. Above all we can forgive each other and pray with each other.

When we find ourselves putting others down and being hard on our-selves, God calls us to be kind and compassionate. We can look at the other person with the forgiving love of Christ. We can stop destructive self-talk with a firm reminder, "Jesus loves me so much he died for me. My sins are gone. If Jesus can forgive me, I can forgive myself."

It's a good way to act until we get to the birthday party that will never end, the one in heaven.

• TOUCH A HEART TODAY •

WATCH FOR A STUDENT WHO ACTS AS A PEACEMAKER OR DOES SOMETHING LOVING FOR ANOTHER CHILD. THANK THAT CHILD FOR BEING KIND AND COMPASSIONATE LIKE JESUS.

It's Midnight and I'm Still Not Ready

Read Psalm 31:15.

The twins had a soccer game. We had to go to the championship celebration at Big John's Pizza. My parents are coming over tomorrow, and I had to pick up the house. Shannon got hysterical because her science project is due Monday, and we had to go buy four AA batteries and copper wire. The washing machine has been running nonstop all day. I finally sit down to prepare my Sunday school lesson as the hands of the clock quickly race toward midnight.

I know what they taught me in teacher meetings. Start planning early. Plan a little bit each day. That works well until life intervenes and I'm bone tired and planning at the last minute again. At times like these, it's good to say with David, "My times are in your hands" (Psalm 31:15).

The Master Teacher got bone tired. Jesus went alone to pray to his Father when he was weary. He longed for a place to rest his head. He even managed to sleep through a threatening storm.

But Jesus calmed that storm when the time was right, and he will calm the storms in your life when the time is right. When you're burning the midnight oil, stop and pray. Let Jesus know you're in a bind. Ask him to give you the energy to plan quickly and efficiently. Ask him to help you get through the next day's lesson successfully and start planning a little earlier next time.

Your times are in God's hands. He knew you before you were born. He knew the proper moment to send his Son to the cross for you. He knows what you've had to accomplish today and still have to accomplish tonight. He'll help you through it.

• TOUCH A HEART TODAY •

IS THERE SOMEONE YOU'VE BEEN THINKING ABOUT CALLING OR VISITING, BUT YOU JUST HAVEN'T FOUND THE TIME? ASK GOD TO HELP YOU FIND THE TIME TODAY.

It Could Snow at Any Time

Read Isaiah 1:18.

Wyatt pulls Karly's chair out from under her just as Karly is about to sit down. Karly ends up on the floor and the class snickers.

"Wyatt, what's wrong with you? Don't you know how dangerous that is? Karly could have been badly hurt!"

Between Wyatt's sin, Karly's blush of embarrassment, and your volcanic explosion of temper, your classroom has become bright scarlet. Thankfully God tells us, "Though your sins are like scarlet, they shall be as white as snow; though they are red as crimson, they shall be like wool" (Isaiah 1:18).

It is the shedding of Jesus' blood on the cross that washes us as clean as snow. It is the power of that redeeming, renewing act that helps us deal firmly but patiently with the Wyatts of the world. It is the refreshment of sins forgiven, as sparkling as new-fallen snow, that helps us get Karly through her embarrassment and back to a comfortable place in class. It is the thought that our own sins nailed Christ to the cross that helps us deal in love with kids who push us to the breaking point.

Try an experiment with your class. Give every student a circle of white paper. Ask them to use a red marker to write down a sin they have recently committed. Then have them fold the circle in half, fold that half-circle in half once again, and fold that quarter in half one last time. Then have them cut notches and patterns along the edges of the folded paper and open it up to create a snowflake. Display your snowflakes—white side up—in your classroom as a constant reminder. Though your sins are as scarlet, they shall be as white as snow.

Pray

Father, thank you for washing me completely clean through the blood of your Son. Help me share that forgiveness with my students. In Jesus' name. Amen.

• TOUCH A HEART TODAY •

SHARE YOUR SNOWFLAKE ACTIVITY WITH A COLLEAGUE. WHEN YOU FEEL HARASSED BY SIN AND TEMPTATION, REMIND EACH OTHER THAT IT COULD SNOW AT ANY TIME.

43

So Who Knew Teachers Have Tests

Read Genesis 22:8.

The doctor wants to try a new procedure.

You got overlooked for a promotion, again.

Your mother can no longer live alone. She needs care 24/7.

A student in your class has Oppositional Defiant Disorder. Things come out of his mouth that you've never heard before.

Pray

Father, thank you for the gift of your Son to understand and help me as I go through life's every trial and temptation. In his name. Amen.

Faith-testing is never pleasant. But in God's hands, it is always triumphant.

Remember how God tested Abraham. God told Abraham to sacrifice his beloved son, Isaac, for whom Abraham and Sarah had longed all of their lives. The request sounds brutal to us, but perhaps not quite so strange to Abraham who witnessed the pagans around him practicing human sacrifice.

As Abraham and Isaac walked to the site God directed, Abraham must have had to hide his tears when his son asked about the lamb for the burnt offering. "God himself will provide the lamb for the burnt offering, my son," Abraham answered (Genesis 22:8).

God has promised never to tempt us beyond what we can endure. He called out to Abraham not to lay a hand on his son and provided a ram for the offering instead. God provided the Lamb for us as well. As Jesus hung on the cross, he suffered the pain of a cancer diagnosis, the loss of employment, the emotional tightrope of raising children while caring for aging parents, and every other kind of human suffering.

Teachers are indeed tested. Jesus walks us through each test, providing answers, comfort, strength, and forgiveness as needed. We'll never take a test alone.

• TOUCH A HEART TODAY •

DO YOU KNOW ANYONE WHO IS GOING THROUGH A TESTING TIME?
OFFER TO PRAY WITH THAT PERSON.

The New Commandment

Read John 13:34.

"**B**rendan, I've told you that you can't get up and sharpen your pencil without permission. I love you."

"Marina, give Javanti's book back and keep your hands to yourself. I love you."

"Patrick, I don't allow that kind of language in this room. I love you."

Well, Jesus does tell us to love everyone, doesn't he? "A new command I give you: Love one another. As I have loved you, so you must love one another" (John 13:34).

The kind of love Jesus is talking about is not a thoughtless, trite, greeting-card love, but a forgiving, life-changing love. Jesus reminded people of their sins, but he also helped them turn their hearts around in repentance.

Pray

Father, you love me so much that you sent your only Son to give his life for me. Help me model that love for my students. In Jesus' name. Amen.

Jesus is our standard for showing love in the classroom. His is a love that embraces every student and understands each student's needs and feelings. His is a love that walks to the cross to take the punishment for every teacher's and every student's sin.

We set classroom standards in love. We reinforce good behavior and correct misbehavior in love. We model Jesus' love in the way we interact with our students. It's a love that lets us love our students even when they're a bit unlovable.

• TOUCH A HEART TODAY •

THINK OF A STUDENT IN YOUR CLASS WHO OFTEN ACTS IN AN "UNLOVABLE" WAY. PRAY FOR THAT STUDENT, AND ASK GOD TO SHOW YOU AN APPROPRIATE WAY TO SHARE HIS LOVE WITH THAT STUDENT.

Do You Glow in the Dark?

Read John 8:12.

Nothing seems gloomier than walking into a classroom that's been decorated for Christmas—one week after Christmas is over. The tree that looked so charming decorated with handmade ornaments is now drooping and dropping needles. The red-and-green paper chains that crisscross the ceiling are now a bother that have to be taken down. Where does the janitor keep the ladder? Even the joy of teaching the story of Christ's birth to be our Savior is done. The crèche set is packed up, and it's back to lessons as usual.

Thankfully, since Christ was born to be our Savior, we never have to teach in an aura of gloom and doom and business as usual. Jesus says, "I am the light of the world. Whoever follows me will never walk in darkness, but will have the light of life" (John 8:12).

> ### Pray
> Father, thank you for sending Jesus to give me the light of life. Help me to reflect his light to my students so that they may feel his brightness. In his name. Amen.

As we bask in Jesus' love, we gratefully reflect his light for all our students to see. It doesn't matter if the weather is gloomy or if the students enter the room in a way that isn't conducive to learning or if you're feeling out of sorts. Jesus' light shines sure and strong.

Jesus' light shining in us gets that room cleaned up and ready for action. Jesus' light shining in us helps us greet students with a glad hello and get them involved in Gospel-filled learning. Jesus' light shines into the hearts of our students and fills them with the certainty of forgiveness and eternal life. You might want to turn off the lights and check it out. You probably do glow in the dark.

• TOUCH A HEART TODAY •

IS A CHILD IN YOUR CLASS GOING THROUGH A ROUGH TIME? GIVE THAT CHILD A SMALL CANDLE OR FLASHLIGHT AS A REMINDER THAT JESUS IS THE LIGHT OF LIFE.

Keep Looking Up!

Read Acts 1:8.

Once there was a kid who was always looking up. Some people thought she was stuck up. Others thought she had a crick in her neck and couldn't straighten it out. Some thought she liked to study cloud formations by day and constellations at night.

Finally someone asked her. "Hey, kid, why are you always looking up?"

"I want to be the first one to see Jesus coming back for us," she answered.

It's not a bad attitude for a Christian. But, along with looking up, Christ has commanded that we do something of great importance while we wait for his return. "You will receive power when the Holy Spirit comes on you; and you will be my witnesses in Jerusalem, and in all Judea and Samaria, and to the ends of the earth" (Acts 1:8).

Pray

Father, keep me looking up to your Son in my attitude, in my faith life, in my energy for teaching your children, and in a wondrous expectation for the time that I may see you face-to-face. In Jesus' name. Amen.

God has filled you with his Holy Spirit so that you can teach the Good News of salvation to the students in your class, to their families as you share what your students are learning, and to the whole world as you organize evangelism projects and support mission work with offerings and prayers.

So keep planning lessons. Keep your head bowed in prayer. But remember to look up, too. You could be the first one to see Jesus coming back.

• TOUCH A HEART TODAY •
LOOK FOR SOMEONE WHO IS LOOKING DOWN IN A DEFEATED WAY.
SEE IF YOU CAN LIFT THAT PERSON UP WITH THE LOVE OF JESUS.

Please Pass the Salt

Read Matthew 5:13.

Salt has a good news/bad news connotation in today's world. Tastes great on popcorn. Wreaks havoc with your blood pressure.

In biblical times, salt was a life-giving commodity. It was used for flavoring food, but—in a hot, arid land that lacked refrigeration—it was also used for preserving food. Salt was even thrown on Old Testament burnt offerings.

When postresurrection Christians hear Jesus say, "You are the salt of the earth" (Matthew 5:13), we know he is motivating us to think of its life-giving properties and be zealous in sharing the Good News of salvation with the students we teach.

Salty teachers prepare lessons that touch their students' lives and get them actively involved in sharing Jesus' love. Salty teachers notice when kids are upset and ask if they'd like to talk for a while. Salty teachers call up parents and let them know the faith-sharing that is going on in their children's lives. Salty teachers notice their colleagues doing a good job and compliment them. Salty teachers know that their students will be in heaven because God's Spirit has chosen to work through us as we speak God's Word of life day by day, lesson by lesson.

Today we know that salt must be used in moderation. But the salt that Jesus compares us to is the life-saving, zesty gift of salvation. Use all you want, all you can!

• TOUCH A HEART TODAY •

EACH TIME YOU REACH FOR THE SALTSHAKER TODAY, PRAY FOR THE STUDENTS IN YOUR CLASS. ASK GOD TO HELP THEM RECEIVE THE GOOD NEWS OF SALVATION IN JESUS WITH READY HEARTS.

I'd Recognize That Voice Anywhere

Read John 10:27–28.

Last summer as I drove through Iowa, I saw a little lamb running along the highway. The rest of the flock was safely housed behind a fence, but this runaway had somehow escaped. Feeling rather Good Shepherd–like, I pulled off the road and got out of my car to call to the lamb. Well, the lamb reacted like I was a shepherd in wolf's clothing. He took off in the opposite direction at top speed. I climbed back in my car, hoping he'd stay off the highway and somehow make his way back into the enclosure.

As I started off, I checked my rearview mirror and started laughing. A man dressed in overalls had climbed out of a pickup truck pulled up to the fence. The entire flock ran in his direction, including my little runaway. The real shepherd scooped up the lamb and put him safely with the flock.

Pray

Father, help me always speak to my students in tones of acceptance and patience. In my Good Shepherd's name. Amen.

That lamb knew his shepherd's voice. Jesus tells us, "My sheep listen to my voice; I know them, and they follow me. I give them eternal life, and they shall never perish" (John 10:27–28). Our students get to know our voices very well. They come to us hoping to hear a welcoming voice of acceptance. When circumstances cause us to speak to our kids with an edge of impatience and irritation, it's time for us to talk to our Good Shepherd.

Jesus knows exactly what's going on in our lives. He knows the endless demands made on our time and emotions. He allows us to rest in his arms and be refreshed. He gently reminds us that he has called us to feed his lambs. And he helps us do it with a warm voice full of love.

• TOUCH A HEART TODAY •

HAS SOMEONE SPOKEN TO YOU RECENTLY IN A WAY THAT LIFTED YOU UP?
TAKE TIME TO THANK THAT PERSON.

Open My Heart:

Prayer and Journal Time

Do some of your colleagues serve as mentors, giving you ideas and encouragement? Thank God for those people. On the hearts on this page, write down some ways you can serve as a cheerleader for your fellow teachers.

Storing Up Treasures in Heaven

Read Matthew 6:19–21.

We Americans tend to have a lot of stuff. When we see the stuff in stores and catalogues and on the Internet, it calls out to us to buy it. We feel we must have it and, when it is first displayed, we look at our new stuff with pleasure. Then our stuff begins to overflow from closets and bookshelves and kids' rooms and threatens to take over the house. From time to time we weed out what we really need from what can be given or thrown away.

Pray

Father, thank you for the many blessings you are helping me store in heaven through the redeeming work of your Son. In his name. Amen.

In his Sermon on the Mount, Jesus told his listeners it was fruitless to store up treasures on earth. They would only be used up, destroyed, or stolen. Instead, he counseled, start storing up treasures in heaven. Only treasures found in heaven last forever.

Christian teachers tend not to be overly tied to status items. Okay, perhaps it's because they can't afford them. But, more likely, they are heeding Jesus' words, "For where your treasure is, there your heart will be also" (Matthew 6:21). The treasure they love is the faith that God's Holy Spirit is planting in the hearts of their students and loved ones.

It's a great blessing to enjoy a comfortable home, good clothes, delicious food, and the newest high-tech items that grab our fancy. But how much more comforting it is to know that because of our teaching—because of our hours of preparation, study, and prayer—young people will one day share a home in heaven with us. That is where our treasure is stored.

• TOUCH A HEART TODAY •

WHO IS SOMEONE YOU TREASURE?
LET THAT PERSON KNOW YOU HOPE YOUR ROOMS WILL BE
NEXT TO EACH OTHER IN HEAVEN.

So Many Words, So Little Time

Read John 20:31.

"We need to take attendance."
"Please don't talk when someone else is talking."
"Be sure to put your chairs up after class."
"Remember to bring back your notes if you can sing in church next Sunday."

We can speak a lot of words to our students and still not get much teaching done. It takes planning, routine, experience, and practice to go from room entry to teaching in one minute flat.

> ### Pray
> Father, let my words be purposeful and invigorating as I share the Gospel with my students. In Jesus' name. Amen.

The same thing can happen when we teach Bible stories. We can get so caught up in where the towns are located on the map and just when the kingdom got divided and how much two mites are worth and why tax collectors were unpopular, that we never get to the meat of the story. John made sure he didn't have that problem. He stated his case like this, "These [miraculous signs] are written that you may believe that Jesus is the Christ, the Son of God, and that by believing you may have life in his name" (John 20:31).

It's a good barometer for our teaching to go over the words we've spoken to our students during the lesson. What percentage dealt with class procedure and discipline? What percentage dealt with factual information? What percentage taught the life-giving lesson that Jesus loved your kids so much that he gave his life on the cross for them?

It's why we teach. That they may have life in his name.

• TOUCH A HEART TODAY •
DO YOU REGULARLY COMMUNICATE WITH SOMEONE WHO IS NOT A CHRISTIAN?
PRAY THAT GOD'S HOLY SPIRIT WILL GIVE YOU ENGAGING WORDS OF WITNESS TO SHARE.

Time and Again

Read John 8:36.

Life is full of addictions. Some are terribly harmful—drugs, pornography, alcohol. Some are unhealthy—coffee, anything that tastes good. Some are time-consuming—TV watching. Some are healthy if not overdone—exercising.

By far our worst addiction is to sin. We're born into it. We can fight it, but it bounces right up to confront us again. That impolite phrase that pops through our mind when someone cuts us off on the freeway. The unkind word that slips out when a spouse or child irritates us. Jealousy. Envy. Hatred. The list is long and biblical.

There is no 12-step program for sin addiction. The program to overcome it took only one step, and Jesus took it for us. Jesus carried all our sins to the cross and suffered the punishment for our wicked addictions. He did it once for all time. "If the Son sets you free, you will be free indeed" (John 8:36).

It isn't easy to teach kids about addiction to sin. We can easily twist the Gospel into Law and have kids thinking, "Jesus wants me to be good. I shouldn't do bad things. Jesus won't love me if I do things that are wrong."

Pray

Father, forgive my sins and help my students feel the freedom of forgiveness your Son won for us. In his name. Amen.

But remember, Jesus has set those kids free, too. They can be thinking, "Jesus loves me even when I forget and do bad things. He'll forgive me and help me to do better." That kind of Gospel-filled teaching gets to be addicting.

• TOUCH A HEART TODAY •
SHARE A "FRIENDLY ADDICTION" WITH A COLLEAGUE—
A CUP OF COFFEE, A MUFFIN, A WORD OF PRAYER.

53

"Thank You, Teacher"

Read Matthew 25:40.

My kids love it when I teach them the meaning of Matthew 25:40. "Sage, one day Jesus is going to say thank you for giving him a drink of water." Sage's eyes are about to pop out of his head. "Remember when you showed that preschool child how to use the drinking fountain? You were really helping Jesus."

The real crowd-pleaser is when Jesus thanks the children for the SpongeBob SquarePants underwear sent in the mission boxes, but we won't go into that now.

Pray

Father, thank you for the knowledge that every act I do in love is really done for your Son. Help me to teach that precious lesson to my students. In Jesus' name. Amen.

Jesus has told us that on the Last Day he will say to us, "I tell you the truth, whatever you did for one of the least of these brothers of mine, you did for me" (Matthew 25:40). One day Jesus will be thanking us for all those Good Samaritan boxes we filled, the canned goods we donated for the food cupboard at church, the toys and blankets we carried to women's shelters, the school supplies we slipped to a child who couldn't afford new ones.

Perhaps the greatest thrill of all is to know that one day Jesus is going to say to us, "Thank you, teacher. Thank you for teaching my children for me. They are here because of you."

And it just might be that the children will say thank you, too.

• TOUCH A HEART TODAY •
SEND A CARD TO SOMEONE IN THE HOSPITAL.
GIVE A LONELY PERSON A CALL. JESUS WILL SAY THANK YOU ONE DAY.

You've Been a Great Class

Read Philippians 1:3.

It has been said that it takes six positive statements to cancel out every negative statement a child hears. Sometimes I stand outside my room after class and listen to the negatives flying from parents to children. "Can't you hurry up? We're late." Or, "Did you bring you book? You're always forgetting it." Or, "No. You can't have ice cream. You didn't clean your room this morning."

Teachers are pretty good at throwing out negative statements of our own. "You were much too noisy in church. You must sit still and listen." Or, "If you can't say something helpful, please don't say anything at all." Or, "How many times have I told you to keep your hands to yourself?"

One wonders if there are enough positive statements in the world to make up for all the negatives our kids hear. Paul had a good handle on it. He told his congregation at Philippi, "I thank my God every time I remember you" (Philippians 1:3). Paul's congregation wasn't made up of perfect saints, only forgiven ones. He was grateful for his followers' participation in the Gospel. They joined him in eagerly learning God's will, in praising God for the gifts of salvation and life in Jesus.

Pray

Father, remind me to speak in positive ways to my students. Let me build them up in your love. In Jesus' name. Amen.

What a great thing to say to our students. "I thank my God every time I remember you." It's a powerful positive, and a true one. These children are about the work of learning God's Word with us. We are leading them in learning God's will for their lives. We are sharing with them the life-giving breath of the Gospel.

At the end of the lesson you can honestly say, "You are a great class. I thank my God every time I remember you."

• TOUCH A HEART TODAY •
WHOM DO YOU THANK GOD FOR EVERY DAY? TELL THAT PERSON SO.

Who Took the Red Paper?

Read 1 Thessalonians 5:16–18.

I'm late. I hit every red light. The kids are going to be running around like wild Indians, and the congregation will think I'm the worst Sunday school teacher who ever lived. Okay. The car is parked. I just have to get some red construction paper out of the supply room so we can cut out our Hearts for Jesus.

"Who took the red construction paper?"

My lamentations can be heard far and wide. I make Job sound like a happy camper.

Mrs. Svarc from next door taps me on the shoulder. "Here's some drawing paper," she says. "You can have the kids color red hearts."

> ### Pray
> Father, help me to remember that joy and thankfulness are not dependant on my circumstances, but on what Christ has done for me. In his name. Amen.

Sometimes Paul's words from Thessalonians come to mind at the oddest times. "Be joyful always; pray continually; give thanks in all circumstances, for this is God's will for you in Christ Jesus" (1 Thessalonians 5:16–18).

Naturally, I'm not happy about being late or running short on supplies. But my happiness does not depend on red construction paper. My joy is a God-given constant in my life. I can be thankful in every circumstance because Jesus gave his life to make me his own. Now we're going to color some red hearts and be thankful about that together.

• TOUCH A HEART TODAY •

LIST THE THINGS YOUR STUDENTS DO THAT MAKE YOU THANKFUL.
READ THE LIST TO THEM THE NEXT TIME YOU SEE THEM.

What Next?

Read Jeremiah 29:11.

I'm not sure if I should keep on teaching. There's plenty to do without it. And there are certainly other ways to serve God.

This hasn't been the best of years. We had to get a new car, and that stretched our budget to the limit. The carpet is getting threadbare, and the clunks from the washing machine are getting louder and stranger. What will we do for money?

Phil's mother really shouldn't be driving anymore. Can I include her errands with my own? And how do we go about talking her out of her last vestige of independence?

What in the world can I do about Kohl? She's getting sneakier and sneakier. She takes stuff out of kids' desks just to get my attention. Should I talk to her mom? to Pastor Greg? Is it enough just to give her more positive attention?

Pray

Father, help me make good decisions about my future. Thank you for making my future in heaven a sure one. In Jesus' name. Amen.

Teachers think such thoughts on a daily basis. Though we keep plenty busy in the present, our minds tend to wander to the future. When that happens, it's helpful to turn to Jeremiah 29:11. "I know the plans I have for you," God assures us, "plans to give you hope and a future."

Your future is sure and certain. God's best plan for you is already set in cement—he sent his Son to die on the cross for you and win you a place beside him in heaven. Think about the future with an open mind. God has only the best in store for you.

• TOUCH A HEART TODAY •

IS A COLLEAGUE OR STUDENT CONCERNED ABOUT MAKING A DECISION? SHARE JEREMIAH 29:11 WITH THAT PERSON.

The Last Day of Teaching

Read Revelation 21:6–7.

There's nothing quite like the last day or session you spend with a class. It's bittersweet. You're looking forward to a little extra time, a break from regular duties. At the same time, you've got these kids where you want them. They're the smartest, funniest, most loving kids you've ever taught. How can you possibly say good-bye?

Think back to the beginning. You've been from A to Z with these kids. You've taught them class routines, expectations, and behaviors. More important, you've taught them the life-giving news that Jesus is their Savior. He lived a perfect life in their place and died to take the punishment for their sins. You can say with a full heart, "Good-bye. If I don't see you soon, I'll see you in heaven."

Pray

Father, thank you for guiding me this year. Bless my students and keep them close to you. In Jesus' name. Amen.

When Jesus shows John a vision of heaven, he says, "It is done. I am the Alpha and the Omega, the Beginning and the End. To him who is thirsty I will give to drink without cost from the spring of the water of life. He who overcomes will inherit all this, and I will be his God and he will be my son" (Revelation 21:6–7).

Jesus is the Alpha and Omega in our teaching. He's been with us from the first day of teaching to the last. We come to him to drink the water of life, and we will never be thirsty again.

• TOUCH A HEART TODAY •

HAS A STUDENT HELPED YOU GROW IN YOUR FAITH LIFE THIS YEAR?
LET THAT STUDENT KNOW HOW YOU FEEL.

Open My Heart:

Prayer and Journal Time

What would you like to change about your teaching in the future? Are there other avenues of ministry in your congregation that you would like to try? Spend some time in God's Word, pray, and jot down your thoughts on the hearts below.

Potato Chips
(For Use at Thanksgiving Time)
Read Luke 6:38.

Isn't it frustrating to open a large bag of potato chips and find that the top half of the bag doesn't contain chips at all? It's just been pumped full of air. Today's material goods tend to be packaged with plenty of filler to make it look like we're getting a lot more than we really are.

Pray
Father, thank you for the blessings you heap upon me. Thank you especially for the gift of eternal life through your Son. In his name. Amen.

That's not the way God does things. He says, "Give, and it will be given to you. A good measure, pressed down, shaken together and running over, will be poured into your lap" (Luke 6:38). In biblical times men wore robes with a fold of material over the front of their belt that could be used as a big pocket. When they went to market, they could buy a big scoop of wheat and carry it home in their pocket.

When God gives, he keeps on giving until the blessings overflow our pockets. You've been giving yourself to the Lord as you teach his children. God readily showers you with blessings.

Enjoy some potato chips today. Each time you bite into a chip, thank God for a blessing he has given you. Family. Health. A job you find fulfilling. Students eager to learn about Jesus. Time to talk with friends. Crisp fall air. Forgiveness for your sins. Eternal life in heaven. You'll run out of chips long before you run out of blessings.

• TOUCH A HEART TODAY •
WRITE A THANK-YOU NOTE TO SOMEONE WHO IS A BLESSING TO YOU.

You Can Trust a Shepherd
(For Use at Christmastime)

Read Luke 2:8–20.

Shepherds didn't have good reputations in biblical times. They were rough, smelly men who spent all their time in the hills with their sheep. Shepherds weren't allowed to be witnesses in a courtroom. They were considered dishonest, untrustworthy.

How interesting that God chose poor, smelly shepherds to be the first witnesses to see his newborn Son. They shook with fear when the bright light of God's angel woke them up while they dozed sleepily, keeping watch over their sheep. But God's angel told the shepherds not to be afraid. God had sent his own Son, Jesus, to be born on earth as a baby so he could be our Savior. Now it was Satan and his wicked angels who shook with fear. Their downfall had begun.

After worshiping at the manger bed that held their newborn Savior and King, the shepherds ran through the streets of Bethlehem telling everybody what they had seen and heard. These scruffy men that nobody trusted became the world's first missionaries.

Christian teaching doesn't rank high on anyone's list of important professions. Christian teachers are rarely seen in the "Newsmakers" page of *Newsweek* or the "Star Tracks" section of *People*. Yet God has chosen us to share the best news of all with his children—Jesus was born to be their Savior.

Interestingly, Jesus is known as a Good Shepherd and the greatest teacher who ever lived. Not bad company for us to be in!

Pray

Father, thank you for choosing me to be a witness to your Son's amazing birth to be our Savior. In his name. Amen.

• TOUCH A HEART TODAY •

WRITE THE NAME OF ONE OF YOUR STUDENTS ON A SCRAP OF PAPER AND HOLD IT IN YOUR HAND WHILE YOU PRAY FOR THAT CHILD. PRAY FOR A DIFFERENT CHILD EACH DAY.

Have a Heart
(For Use on Valentine's Day)

Read John 15:13.

A priest named Valentine was killed in Rome on February 14 in A.D. 270 because of his love for Jesus. We don't know much else about St. Valentine. No one knows why people started sending each other cards on February 14 and calling them "Valentines."

We know the name of another person who was killed for love. His name is Jesus. Jesus said, "Greater love has no one than this, that he lay down his life for his friends" (John 15:13). The cross tells us more about real love than any Valentine.

The meaning of the name *Valentine* is something of a mystery, but there's no mystery at all about Jesus' name. Gabriel told Joseph, "Do not be afraid to take Mary home as your wife, because what is conceived in her is from the Holy Spirit. She will give birth to a son, and you are to give him the name Jesus, because he will save his people from their sins" (Matthew 1:20-21). *Jesus* is a Greek word that means "the Lord saves."

Teachers celebrate Valentine's Day all year long. Each time we stand before our students, we tell them about the love of Jesus—a love so great that he was willing to save us from sin, death, and the power of the devil.

Happy Valentine's Day in Jesus' name!

• TOUCH A HEART TODAY •

LOOK AT SOME CANDY CONVERSATION HEARTS WITH YOUR STUDENTS.
SEE IF THEY CAN THINK OF WAYS IN WHICH THE SAYINGS REMIND THEM OF JESUS.

What's in Your Basket?
(For Use during the Easter Season)

Read 1 Corinthians 15:17, 20.

Do you make a habit of filling Easter baskets for your family? The days when colored eggs and fake green grass did the trick are long gone. Today's Easter baskets tend to contain toys and gifts that overshadow the traditional chocolate bunnies and marshmallow chicks.

An Easter basket that God might fill for us would contain some powerful gifts. Paul says, "If Christ has not been raised, your faith is futile; you are still in your sins" (1 Corinthians 15:17). If Jesus had stayed in the tomb, our faith would be useless. Jesus would be known as a good teacher who seemed able to do magical things. Our lives would be spent in hopeless worry over sin, death, and what might happen next. Our faith would be useless.

But Paul goes on to say, "Christ has indeed been raised from the dead, the firstfruits of those who have fallen asleep" (1 Corinthians 15:20). God the Father did raise Jesus from the dead! Our faith is useful, and our Easter basket is brimming with gifts—new life in Christ, forgiveness for our sins, unconditional love from God, the promise of eternal life in heaven.

Write these gifts on cards and place them in an Easter basket. Let your students take turns pulling the cards out of the basket and reading them. Pray together as you thank God for your full Easter basket. It holds enough forgiveness, love, and faith to last for all eternity.

Pray

Father, thank you for sending Jesus to die and rise for me. Thank you for the privilege of being able to share this Good News with the students I teach. In Jesus' name. Amen.

• TOUCH A HEART TODAY •

ASK YOUR STUDENTS TO MAKE EASTER CARDS FOR HOSPITALIZED AND HOMEBOUND MEMBERS OF YOUR CONGREGATION.